ARMIES OF THE PAST

GOING TO WAR IN
VICTORIAN TIMES

ARMIES OF THE PAST

GOING TO WAR IN
VICTORIAN
TIMES

CRAIG DODD

W
FRANKLIN WATTS
LONDON•SYDNEY

ILLUSTRATIONS BY

Mark Bergin
Kevin Maddison
Lee Montgomery
Nick Spender
Peter Visscher
Mike White
Maps by Stefan Chabluk

Editor Penny Clarke
Editor-in-Chief John C. Miles

Designer Steve Prosser
Art Director Jonathan Hair/Jason Anscomb
Picture Research Susan Mennell

© 2001 Franklin Watts

First published in 2001
by Franklin Watts
96 Leonard Street
London
EC2A 4XD

Franklin Watts Australia
56 O'Riordan Street
Alexandria
NSW 2015

ISBN 0 7496 4041 3

Dewey classification: 909.81

A CIP catalogue record
for this book is available
from the British Library.

Printed in Hong Kong, China

CONTENTS

THE WORLD 1850-80

Many people imagine that, apart from a few local conflicts, the peace that followed the end of the Napoleonic Wars in 1815 lasted until World War One broke out in 1914. They are wrong. Throughout the 19th century soldiers were constantly in action somewhere in the world, especially in the years 1850-80.

On mainland Europe, in the Balkans, in India and Africa, in North and South America and the Far East armies fought each other. These conflicts resulted in the deaths of thousands. Many thousands more died later of their wounds. Disease, however, was the biggest killer: camps and hospitals were full of germs.

This book looks at army life in the third quarter of the 19th century: the period when all the conflicts listed below were fought.

UNION STATES OF AMERICA

American Civil War 1861-65

CONFEDERATE STATES OF AMERICA

Abraham Lincoln (1809-65) Elected US President in 1860, Abraham Lincoln steered the Union states to victory in the Civil War. Just six weeks before the Confederate states finally surrendered, he was shot dead by John Wilkes Booth.

MAJOR CONFLICTS 1850-80

War in the Crimea
In 1854, war broke out on the Crimean Peninsula after the Tsar (Emperor) of Russia claimed Ottoman (Turkish) territory. This would have given the Russian navy access to the Mediterranean Sea. Desperate to avoid this threat, France and Britain sent troops; for two years the Crimean War raged.

Mutiny in India
In 1857, the British East India Company issued its Indian soldiers with ammunition smeared with grease made from cow and pig fat. As cows are sacred to Hindus and Muslims cannot eat pork, soldiers of both religions were offended and they mutinied. The Indian Mutiny lasted for more than a year before it was suppressed.

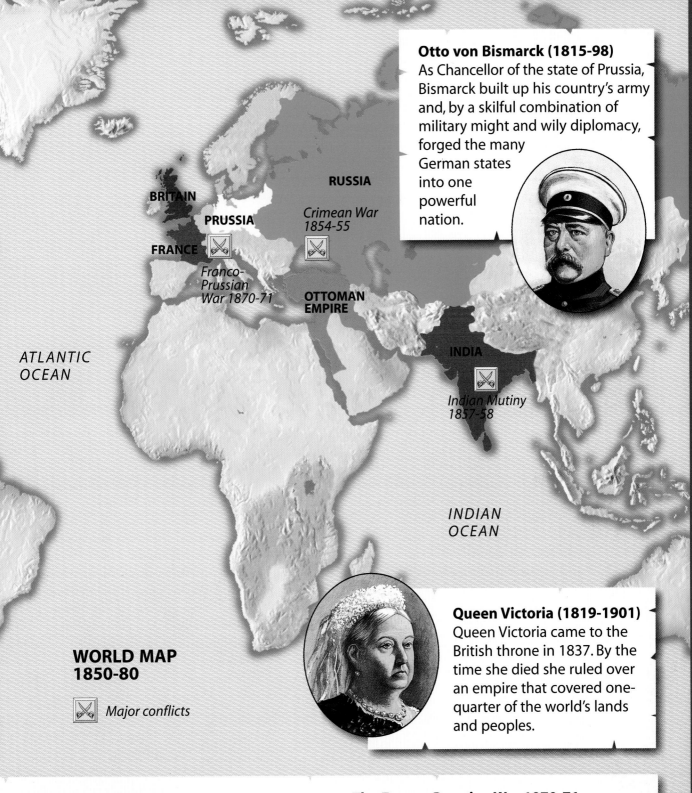

Otto von Bismarck (1815-98)
As Chancellor of the state of Prussia, Bismarck built up his country's army and, by a skilful combination of military might and wily diplomacy, forged the many German states into one powerful nation.

RUSSIA

BRITAIN

PRUSSIA

Crimean War 1854-55

FRANCE

Franco-Prussian War 1870-71

OTTOMAN EMPIRE

ATLANTIC OCEAN

INDIA

Indian Mutiny 1857-58

INDIAN OCEAN

WORLD MAP 1850-80

Major conflicts

Queen Victoria (1819-1901)
Queen Victoria came to the British throne in 1837. By the time she died she ruled over an empire that covered one-quarter of the world's lands and peoples.

The Un-United States

In 1860, the American state of South Carolina declared that the union between itself and the rest of the United States was at an end. Other southern states followed, and formed themselves into a Confederacy. The American Civil War began the next year; it ripped apart the United States for four terrible years.

The Franco-Prussian War 1870-71

In 1870 the German state of Prussia provoked France into declaring war, hoping to encourage smaller states to join the Prussian-dominated North German Federation. After eight months, the French surrendered, leaving Germany the most powerful country on mainland Europe.

RECRUITING

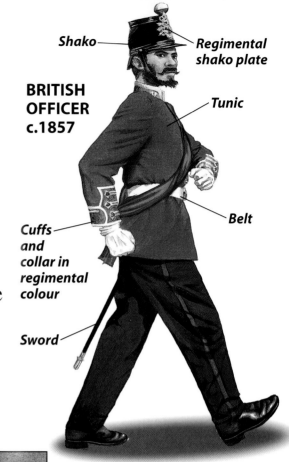

BRITISH OFFICER c.1857

Shako

Regimental shako plate

Tunic

Belt

Cuffs and collar in regimental colour

Sword

W ith wars breaking out and growing empires to patrol, 19th-century governments needed to recruit (sign up) young men for their armies. Army recruiters were happy to tell likely lads how wonderful it was to be a soldier.

The truth was rather different. Peacetime soldiers did little except drill; in war they were killed by enemy gunfire or disease. If the army offered a bounty (cash payment) on joining up, it rarely covered the cost of necessities such as clothing.

ARMY OFFICERS

Being an officer was a good career, especially for younger sons of wealthy families. In Britain, such a family could, until 1871, buy a commission (job as an officer).

Things were different in the democratic United States. In the US Civil War some groups of recruits elected their officers.

RECRUITING SERGEANTS

In Britain, army recruiting sergeants bought young men beer in the village pub or at the local fair. They told the boys (often teenagers) how the army offered a chance to see the world and how girls loved a man in uniform.

LOCAL LOYALTIES

Armies in the 19th century were organised into large groups of men, called regiments. The numbers of men within a regiment varied. The British army contained regiments with names such as the Lancashire Fusiliers. These names reflected the region of Britain where the unit was raised.

Regimental badge of the Lancashire Fusiliers

COMPULSORY SERVICE IN EUROPE

In the 1860s, as part of his army reforms in Prussia, Bismarck introduced compulsory military service for all men of suitable age. And so for a short period of their lives every young man in the country, with few exemptions, had to undergo military training. By the 1870s Prussia had a pool of more than 700,000 trained men.

NUMBERS GAME

France had a different system. Every French man was given a number; those whose numbers came up were conscripted into the army for up to seven years. Those who 'drew a bad number' could pay for a substitute (often someone in desperate need of money) to take their place.

French soldier c.1860

Prussian soldier c.1870

Wide-brimmed hat

Musket

Blanket roll

Water canteen

CONFEDERATE CONSCRIPT, 1862

🔔 MILITIAMEN

Before the US Civil War, the Federal government encouraged each state to form a militia unit.

Militiamen were part-time civilian volunteers who got together regularly to drill and practise shooting. If war broke out they would form the core of each fighting unit.

🔔 NORTH AND SOUTH

When the US Civil War began, young men flocked to volunteer for their local militia. Most Civil War soldiers were volunteers, but the Confederate states introduced conscription in 1862, forcing men of suitable age to join up.

Union states introduced recruitment quotas that each state had to meet. Both sides allowed men to avoid military service by paying an annual tax.

COMMANDERS

In a monarchy, the king or queen is usually head of the armed services. During the 19th century some, such as Queen Victoria, played a ceremonial role. Others, such as Napoleon III of France and Wilhelm I of Prussia, took a more active part, discussing tactics with their generals and appointing senior officers.

In the United States the president is the commander-in-chief of the armed forces. During the US Civil War, Abraham Lincoln was very active in this role; his generals were well aware that it was the president who was in command.

A British fusilier

WEST POINT
Many Civil War senior officers trained at the US military academy at West Point. Among them were Ulysses S. Grant, commander of the Union army, and Robert E. Lee, who commanded the Confederate forces.

GENERAL GRANT
At the outbreak of the US Civil War, an ex-US army officer offered his services to the Union army. Ulysses S. Grant led the Union army to victory over the Confederacy and later became president of the USA.

PRIVATE GENTLEMEN
The lowest rank in any army was private, short for 'private gentleman'. Different regiments had different names for privates. In Britain, for example, a private in a Guards regiment was called a 'guardsman', in a Fusilier regiment a 'fusilier' or in a cavalry regiment a 'trooper'.

A Union general in the US Civil War

(Right) General Ulysses S. Grant

WHO WAS WHO IN THE BRITISH ARMY, 1860

In the 19th-century British army, every man knew his place. Here are some of the ranks then – and now.

The highest rank an officer could achieve was field marshal, a title dating from 1736. Field marshals commanded entire armies.

Below the rank of field marshal came generals. Generals directed movements of troops to and on the field of battle rather than commanding individual regiments. That was the responsibility of colonels in infantry regiments and lieutenant-colonels in artillery and cavalry regiments.

Sub-units within each regiment were in the charge of commissioned officers, such as majors and captains, who were assisted by more junior officers, such as lieutenants.

Below these ranks were warrant officers. The regimental sergeant-major was responsible for all aspects of discipline in the ranks. Sergeants commanded small groups of men in action, ensuring the officers' orders were carried out.

Next came two ranks of non-commissioned officer: corporals and lance-corporals who in turn were senior to the lowest rank of trained soldier, the private (gunner in the Royal Regiment of Artillery, trooper in a cavalry regiment).

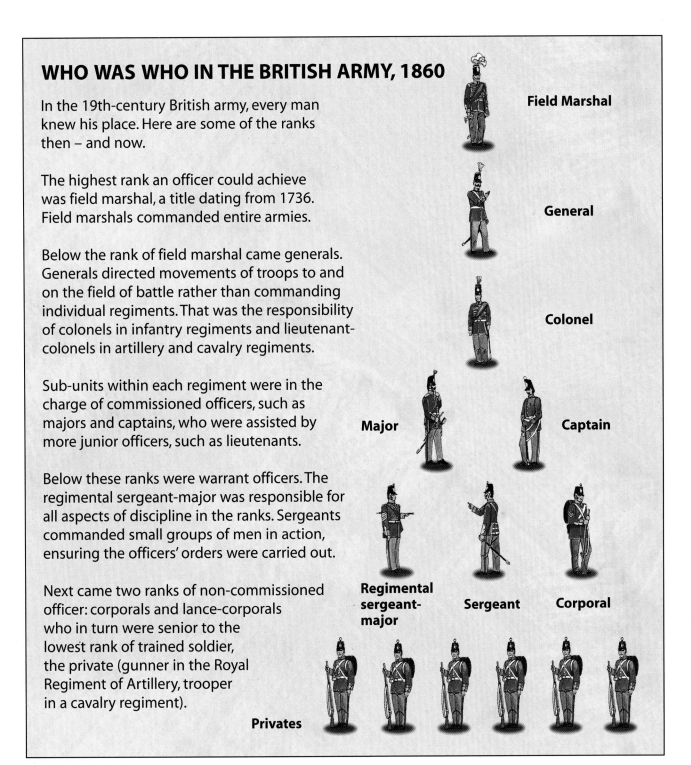

Field Marshal

General

Colonel

Major

Captain

Regimental sergeant-major

Sergeant

Corporal

Privates

THE REGIMENT

The basic unit of all armies of the period was the regiment. In both Europe and the United States regiments recruited in the areas in which they were based. During the US Civil War, recruits who enlisted in their local militia found that their units were incorporated into a larger regiment. In Britain, men enlisted in a regiment and usually stayed in the same unit until their spell of duty came to an end.

HOME AND ABROAD

With a large empire to patrol, British regiments were usually divided into two parts, one serving abroad while the other stayed at home. Regiments in the US Civil War were on active service throughout the conflict.

UNIFORMS

Wearing a uniform encouraged a soldier to act as part of a team. If he wore exactly the same clothes as his comrades, he was more likely to identify with them and be happier to march into action alongside them.

Uniforms also made soldiers easier to distinguish: that's why the uniforms of different regiments varied even if it was in such a small detail as how the buttons were arranged on a soldier's tunic.

US CIVIL WAR UNION SOLDIER

- Kepi (cap)
- Rolled blanket and backpack
- Tunic
- Cartridge pouch
- Belt
- Haversack
- Tin cup
- Muzzle-loading musket

A Union soldier recalls altering uniforms in the US Civil War:

'It was clear that Uncle Sam's tailor had no idea of measuring the man and then fitting his suit … nor were the seams of these new garments always equal to the strain to which they were subjected, so that in the course of the first week after they were donned, many of the wearers had to resort to the sewing kit thoughtfully provided by a loving wife or mother.'

THE BLUES AND THE GREYS

Uniforms worn by US Civil War soldiers varied in detail from regiment to regiment but, in general, Union soldiers wore dark blue coats with lighter blue trousers and kepis (round, peaked caps). Cavalrymen wore short jackets.

Confederate forces mostly wore grey coats and caps with blue or brown trousers. As the war progressed and supplies grew scarcer, many infantrymen were forced to wear drab brown uniforms made of roughly woven material that was uncomfortable against the skin.

HEADGEAR

19th-century Prussian helmet

PRUSSIA

From around 1835 Prussian soldiers wore helmets with decorative spikes, something the French army adopted after its defeat in the Franco-Prussian War.

FRENCH

French soldiers, like their British counterparts, wore a hat called a shako. It was a cylindrical, flat-topped hat made of leather. It had a small peak and a coloured pompom mounted centrally.

Pompom

19th-century French shako

Confederate army kepi

AMERICAN

Most US Union soldiers wore a soft cap with a stiffened peak. This type of headgear was called a 'kepi'. Confederate troops wore a grey, broad-brimmed hat or kepi with a blue band.

British soldier in an 1850s khaki uniform.

THE COLOUR OF DUST

At first, British troops serving in India wore the same style of uniform as their comrades in Europe. But soldiers found that woollen tunics were too heavy to wear in tropical heat. So, from the 1850s, they began to have their uniforms made in lighter cloth such as khaki drill cotton. The word 'khaki' means 'dust-coloured' in Urdu. The colour of their new uniforms merged into the landscape and made soldiers more difficult for the enemy to spot.

Victoria Cross

Medal of Honor

'FOR VALOUR'

Between 1850 and 1880 two of the most famous of all military medals were introduced. In 1856 Queen Victoria instituted the Victoria Cross. It is Britain's highest military decoration and is inscribed with the words 'For Valour'.

The United States' highest military medal is the Medal of Honor. It is awarded to servicemen for bravery beyond the call of duty in direct action with the enemy. It is awarded by the president in the name of Congress, so it is often called (incorrectly) the Congressional Medal of Honor.

TOO BRIGHT FOR SAFETY

During the 19th century army commanders began to realise that soldiers in brightly coloured tunics were easy targets for enemy snipers. By 1890, most countries had introduced more sober colours for the uniforms their soldiers wore in action.

INFANTRY

A British infantryman loads his musket.

In a 19th-century battle, the role of the infantry was to break through and create gaps in the lines of enemy soldiers. In the early 1800s the usual tactic was for infantry to fire one or two rounds from their muzzle-loading muskets. Then each man fixed a bayonet on his gun and waited for the order to charge at the enemy.

By the time of the Franco-Prussian War in 1870, armies had begun to acquire breech-loading guns that could be fired lying down. These were much quicker to reload and fire. As a result, tactics changed and bayonet charges became obsolete.

Ramrod pushes the charge down the barrel.

GEAR

Cutlery

Canteen

Backpack

Mug

Tin dish

Cartridge bag

Haversack for food

INFANTRY KIT
US Civil War infantry marched into battle laden with equipment. Their rifles weighed nearly five kilos and their field packs more than four times that. They also had to find room for their cartridge boxes and personal effects.

MUZZLE-LOADERS
The guns used by infantry in the early 1800s were called muzzle-loaders because they were loaded from the muzzle (front end) of the gun.

Each soldier pushed a cartridge containing the gunpowder charge and lead ball down the barrel with a metal ramrod (above). This process could be dangerous, as it exposed the soldier to enemy fire.

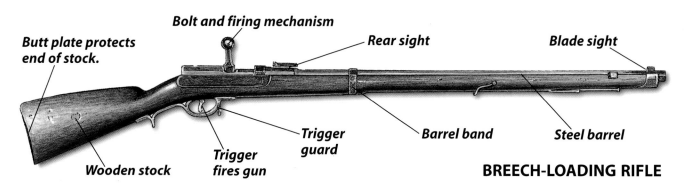

Butt plate protects
end of stock.

Bolt and firing mechanism

Rear sight

Blade sight

Wooden stock

Trigger
fires gun

Trigger
guard

Barrel band

Steel barrel

BREECH-LOADING RIFLE

BREECH-LOADERS

An important step in the
evolution of breech-loading
guns – ones that load from the
breech (rear) end of the barrel
– was the invention of the self-
contained cartridge. This
included in one package the
bullet, explosive propellant
powder and detonator.

In 1827, inventor Johannes von
Dreyse persuaded Prussian
generals to adopt his design for
this. Ten years later, von Dreyse
used his cartridges in a gun he
had invented. Called the
Needle gun because of its
needle-shaped firing pin, it
was the first practical breech-
loading rifle.

*French troops fire Chassepot
rifles in the Franco-Prussian War.*

Johannes von Dreyse

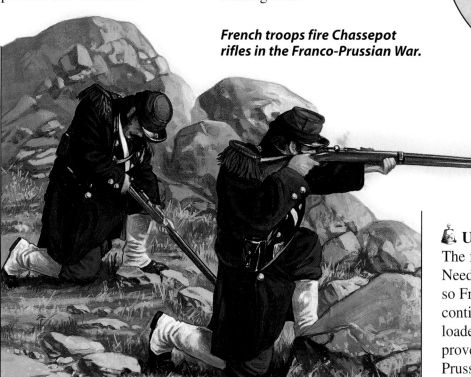

A BETTER WEAPON

The first widely manufactured military breech-loading rifle was
the French 'Chassepot', introduced in 1866. Named after its
inventor, M. Chassepot, the gun was much more reliable and
accurate than the Prussian Needle gun. During the Franco-Prussian
War, the Prussian army armed its snipers with Chassepots, which
they took from captured or dead French infantrymen.

UNRELIABLE WONDER

The firing mechanism of the
Needle gun was unreliable,
so French and British armies
continued using muzzle-
loaders. But the Needle gun
proved valuable in the Austro-
Prussian War of 1866 and the
Franco-Prussian War of 1870.

CIVIL WAR RIFLES

In the United States, companies
such as Hall, Joslyn and Jenks
were at the forefront of making
breech-loaders, and their rifles
were used by both sides during
the Civil War.

ARTILLERY

The 'Dictator'

Big guns – artillery – have been used by armies for centuries. The first recorded use was in the 14th century.

Early artillery worked in a straightforward way – explosive gunpowder rammed into the barrel of the cannon was ignited to propel the cannonball out of the gun.

During the 19th century – as happened with smaller, hand-held weapons – breech-loading was made a practical possibility. As a result artillery became much more efficient.

BIG AND SMALL

Some artillery was light enough to be mounted on gun carriages that could be pushed or pulled into position by one or two soldiers. Heavier guns were horse-drawn.

Some big guns, such as the 'Dictator', a mortar used by the Union army during the Civil War, were so gigantic that they had to be mounted on railway wagons.

LOADING AND FIRING A CANNON

READY...
First, the gun's crew rammed a cloth bag of gunpowder and a cannonball down the barrel.

AIM...
Then the gunner aimed the gun, pierced the cartridge and poured gunpowder into the touchhole.

FIRE!
When this was ignited, the charge in the barrel exploded and the ball flew towards the enemy.

AMMUNITION

Wooden base made loading easier.

Solid round shot

Explosive shells

Shrapnel shell was filled with lead balls.

Case shot contained iron balls.

Grape shot

Big guns used many deadly types of ammunition. The most common was solid round shot. There were also hollow shells, filled with explosive, that blew up when they hit their target.

Grape shot consisted of a cluster of about 12 small iron balls that flew apart on firing and wrought havoc.

Case shot was a sphere filled with musket balls. And shrapnel shells exploded in mid-air to rain down death on the enemy.

🔥 RAPID FIRE

As the 19th century progressed, most armies developed quick-firing breech-loading artillery. The first successful breech-loading big gun was made at the Krupps works at Essen, Germany, in the 1860s.

By the end of the century artillery such as the French 75 mm field gun could fire up to 20 rounds per minute.

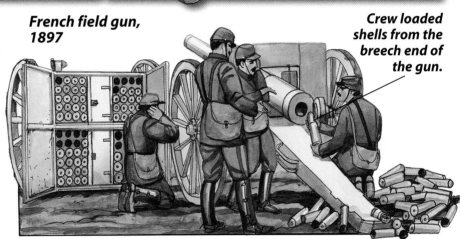

French field gun, 1897

Crew loaded shells from the breech end of the gun.

An 1870s Prussian gun crew aim a field gun.

🔥 THE GUNNERS

Many guns were horse-drawn, but even so the horses could only take the guns so far and then human brawn had to take over. Artillerymen had to be strong enough to pull their guns to where they were needed.

With each shot the force of the explosion moved the gun. This meant that gunners had to push and pull their gun back into position and re-aim it each time.

ON THE MOVE

Armies of the early 1800s often marched thousands of miles to battle. British troops on their way to the Crimea and India in the 1850s didn't have a long march – they were transported by ship.

US Civil War soldiers did endure some long marches, but both sides transported troops on the United States' growing network of railways. As the century progressed, trains became more important in war, playing a big part in Prussia's victory over France in 1871.

A COSTLY MISTAKE

France, unlike Prussia, paid scant attention to using railways for military purposes until it was too late. In the Franco-Prussian War, French troop trains ran late, jammed lines and often dropped soldiers a long way from the action.

A French troop train

TROOPSHIP TO INDIA

During the 19th century, the only way to get soldiers from Britain to India was by ship. Soldiers faced a two-month voyage in crowded and filthy conditions (below). Many died en route and were buried at sea.

18

BETTER LINKS

In the United States, there were more railways in the northern states than there were in the south. This gave the Union army an advantage in moving their men and artillery to where they were needed.

That's not to say that the south didn't use railways, too. At the first Battle of Bull Run in 1861, the Confederates brought in extra troops by train and this swung the battle in their favour.

The General

THE *GENERAL*

In April 1862 Captain James Andrews and a group of Union soldiers seized a Confederate steam locomotive, the *General,* at Shanty in Confederate Georgia. They drove it for 140 km until it ran out of steam and it was recaptured by Confederate troops who had been chasing it. Andrews and his men were executed: the *General* went back on duty transporting troops.

A soldier from Pennsylvania remembers setting off for the US Civil War by train:

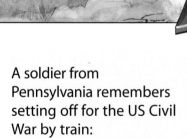

'As the train pulled out we all turned to take one last look at the familiar scenes. Many a hearty cheer was wafted to the boys, and then the sad and weeping friends and families moved off to their homes, feeling that there was a vacant chair at the fireside that perhaps would never again be filled by the absent one.'

ARMOURED MONSTER

As soon as generals realised that railways could be useful in wartime, many new railway-based inventions were developed. The rail car shown below was used in the US Civil War and mounted a cannon. The crew was protected by armour plating.

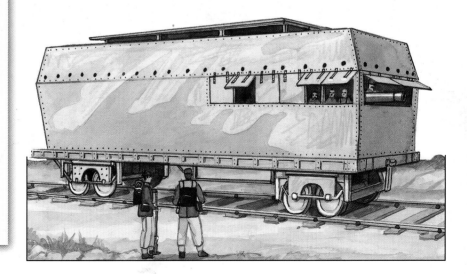

CAVALRY

Cavalry – soldiers on horseback – played many roles in the 19th-century army. They observed and reported information about the enemy and covered the movements of their own infantry and artillery. Their charges demoralised the enemy, especially if they were sudden attacks on weak points. Finally, towards the end of a battle, cavalry pursued fleeing enemy soldiers.

As the 19th century progressed, cavalry became vulnerable as a result of the introduction of quick-firing rifles and machine guns. One of the last great cavalry charges of the 1800s occurred in the Franco-Prussian War.

Lord Raglan, commander-in chief of the British army in the Crimea

FATAL CHARGE

At the Battle of Balaclava in 1854, 637 men of the British Light Brigade (cavalry) were ordered to attack Russian guns.

The British troops galloped along a valley to reach their objective but could not hold it without support. So they turned around and galloped back again. Nearly 250 men were killed or badly injured.

The Light Brigade charges at Balaclava

KITTED OUT

PISTOLS AND SABRES

Cavalry troopers carried a large amount of equipment with them as they rode into battle. This included weapons such as pistols and long slashing swords called sabres.

Cavalry sabre

Cavalry pistol

Officer's .44- calibre revolver

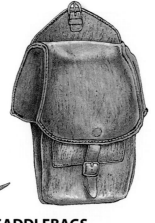

SADDLEBAGS

A trooper's saddlebags contained grooming kit for his horse, pen and paper, books including probably a Bible, and other personal effects.

BLANKET ROLL AND CANTEEN

Troopers carried their blanket rolls and water canteens strapped to their saddles. Often they carried a greatcoat as well.

Canteen

Blanket roll

🔔 CHARGE!

There were three divisions in a cavalry regiment – assault, support and reserve. On the command, 'Walk-march' the assault and support divisions moved slowly forwards.

When they were about 700 metres from enemy lines, they started to trot. Just 180 metres from the enemy, the assault troops hurled themselves into a charge.

🔔 CAVALRY IN THE US CIVIL WAR

The Confederates had a huge number of expert horsemen who had learnt their skills hunting, This gave them a head start in cavalry tactics – a lead they maintained for the first half of the war.

Despite the large number of cavalry north and south, cavalry battles as such were few and far between. Commanders preferred to use horsemen for reconnaissance, to screen infantry formations and to make deceptive manoeuvres intended to confuse the enemy.

A Confederate soldier describes a Union cavalry charge in the US Civil War:

'Halloo! Here comes a cavalry charge from the Yankee line. They thunder down upon us. Their slat-footed dragoons shale and jar the earth. They are all around us. We are surrounded!'

A Union cavalry trooper of the US Civil War

LIFE IN CAMP

The Crimean War lasted for 22 months during which there were only three major battles – the Alma, Balaclava and Inkerman. For British soldiers the war meant weeks, sometimes months, in field camps – drilling, scouting or simply waiting to march into battle.

It was different for soldiers fighting in the US Civil War. From April 1861 to May 1865 there were more than 230 battles. Some were little more than skirmishes, others were full-scale battles with artillery and infantry attacks followed by cavalry charges. But despite all this action, soldiers still spent a long time in camp, eating, gambling or simply waiting.

DRILLING

New recruits usually did their initial training in the regimental barracks before being sent into action. For all soldiers this meant long hours of drill (practising various manoeuvres).

Boring it may have been, but drilling turned soldiers into a team and instilled a sense of pride in the unit.

Prussian soldier drilling

OFF DUTY

In their spare time, many soldiers drank and played cards. If they were literate, they read books and wrote letters home. Sometimes women and children travelled with the army.

A Union soldier and family at Camp Slocum, near Washington DC, in 1862

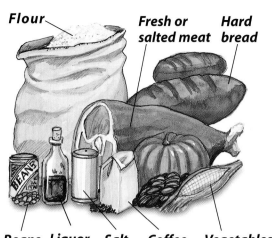

Flour

Fresh or salted meat

Hard bread

Beans Liquor Salt Coffee Vegetables

A SOLDIER'S DAY
5.00 am Wakened by a drummer or bugler.
5.15 am Washed and dressed, present for roll call.
5.30 am Breakfast.
6.00 am Chopping firewood, cleaning camp and other general duties.
8.00 am Guard duty inspection. Each soldier on 24-hour guard duty expected to stand on duty for two hours out of every six. Drilling.
Noon Dinner.
2.00 pm Drilling.
4.30 pm Preparation for evening inspection.
5.45 pm Retreat, roll call, inspection and dress parade.
6.30 pm Supper.
8.30 pm Last roll call; lights out at 9 pm.

RATIONS

In the 1860s, the emphasis in a soldier's diet was on bulk rather than flavour. Above is a Union soldier's weekly ration. This was much better than the food British soldiers fighting in the Crimea a few years earlier had to endure: their usual meal was a thin stew of stringy beef and potatoes.

SAME AGAIN...

A soldier's life could be very boring. Above is a typical infantryman's day in camp.

Union soldiers raid a farm for pigs and chickens.

LIVING OFF THE LAND!

Like their comrades in European armies of the time, Union and Confederate soldiers tried to break the monotony of their diet by foraging for whatever they could. Some men hunted wild game in the woods. Others stole chickens and pigs from farms.

A guest at a farm recalls foraging troops:

'During supper women came rushing in at intervals saying, "Oh good heavens, now they're killing our fat hogs! Which is the General? Our milk cows are now going!" General Longstreet replied, "Yes, madam, it's very sad. This sort of thing has been going on in Virginia for more than two years – very sad."'

WAR AT SEA

Throughout the 19th century the British navy was the strongest in the world. Prussia's Chancellor Bismarck and Napoleon III of France were more concerned with building up their armies than strengthening their navies. So European sailors played only a relatively small part in military matters in the years 1850-80.

It was a different story during the American Civil War, when a new type of warship – the ironclad – steamed into battle.

The crew of an ironclad relax on deck during the US Civil War.

Britain's first ironclad warship was HMS Warrior, 1860.

FIRST IRONCLADS
The first ironclad was the French *La Gloire* of 1859, closely followed by Britain's HMS *Warrior* in 1860. Both ships had stout wooden hulls covered with iron armour plate. Neither saw action. HMS *Warrior* is preserved today at Portsmouth.

IRON GOES TO WAR
A few days into the US Civil War, Confederate forces captured a Union ship, the USS *Merrimack*, and renamed it the CSS *Virginia*. They covered it with iron plating and fitted an iron ram to its bows. Once its engine had been repaired and it had been re-armed with ten cannon, the south had a formidable new weapon.

BATTLE OF THE TITANS

When the citizens of Washington DC heard that the Confederate navy now had an iron warship they feared that it would sail up the Potomac River and shell the city. So the US navy commissioned an ironclad of its own, the USS *Monitor*. The *Monitor* entered service on 25 February 1862. Eleven days later, the *Virginia* led an attack on a US naval squadron, sinking one ship, destroying another and forcing a third to run aground.

FOUR-HOUR BATTLE

The following day, 9 March 1862, the *Virginia* and the *Monitor* sailed into range of each other's artillery. For four hours, their big guns bombarded each other before the ships' commanders decided to call it a draw and steamed off.

The battle between the Monitor *and the* Virginia *in 1862*

CSS *Virginia*

USS *Monitor*

A *Monitor* crew member recalls how the captain was injured on 9 March 1862:

'Soon after noon a shell from the enemy's gun struck the forward side of the pilot-house. The captain was standing immediately behind the spot and received in his face the full force of the blow. He was a ghastly sight ... I assisted in leading him to his cabin where he was cared for by Doctor Logue and then I assumed command.'

THE *MONITOR'S* TURRET

The *Monitor* was designed by the brilliant Swedish-American engineer John Ericsson. It was armed with two huge 280-mm cannon. These were contained in an armoured turret that could be swivelled to point the guns in any direction. This arrangement led the way for battleship designs of the later 1800s.

CROSS-SECTION OF THE *MONITOR'S* TURRET

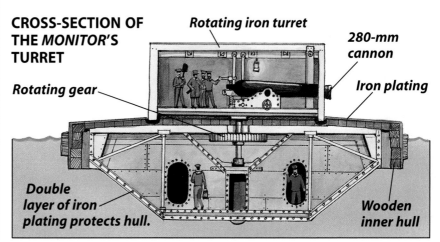

Rotating iron turret

280-mm cannon

Iron plating

Rotating gear

Double layer of iron plating protects hull.

Wooden inner hull

MEDICINE

No one knows exactly how many soldiers were killed in battle in the mid-19th century. But it was less than the number who died of illnesses and infections.

When the Crimean War started, military hospitals were filthy. There were not enough beds: wounded and desperately ill soldiers lay on the floor watching comrades having shattered limbs amputated without anaesthetic.

Conditions started to get better when a dedicated nurse called Florence Nightingale arrived in the Crimea. By the end of the century medical care had improved greatly.

ANGEL OF MERCY

When Florence Nightingale (above) arrived in the Crimea to nurse injured soldiers she was appalled by conditions. She and her nurses worked 20 hours a day; gradually death rates fell.

While her exhausted nurses slept, she toured the wards carrying a lamp and talking to the injured. It was this that gave her the nickname 'The Lady with the Lamp'.

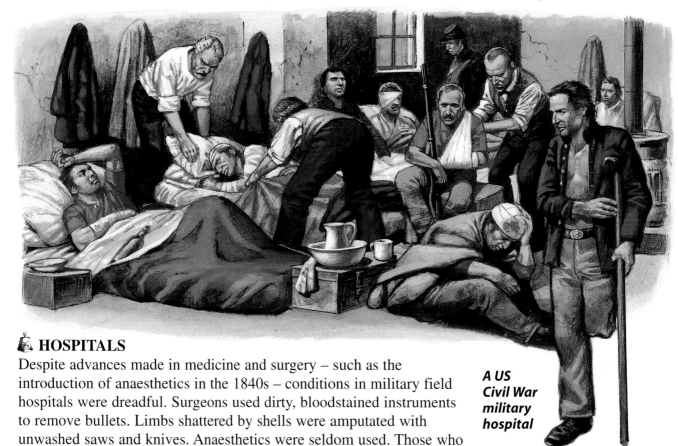

HOSPITALS

Despite advances made in medicine and surgery – such as the introduction of anaesthetics in the 1840s – conditions in military field hospitals were dreadful. Surgeons used dirty, bloodstained instruments to remove bullets. Limbs shattered by shells were amputated with unwashed saws and knives. Anaesthetics were seldom used. Those who survived the surgeon's knife were more often than not killed by fevers.

A US Civil War military hospital

SURGICAL KIT

Army doctors had a range of instruments available to help them deal with different types of injury. There were knives to cut through flesh, saws to cut bone, probes and bullet extractors. Here is a surgeon's kit from the 1850s.

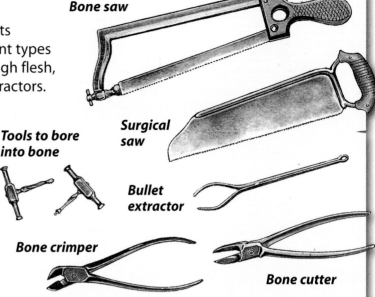

Bone saw

Surgical saw

Tools to bore into bone

Bullet extractor

Probe

Scalpel

Surgeon's mallet

Bone crimper

Bone cutter

Amputation knife

Henri Dunant with the flag of the Red Cross

One US soldier who survived having an arm amputated later wrote:

'I asked if there was any chloroform, to which the surgeon replied, "No, and I have no time to dilly-dally with you." Then they finished the job and I was led away a short distance and left to lie on the hot sand.'

THE RED CROSS

In 1859, during the short Franco-Austrian War, a Swiss businessman, Henri Dunant, witnessed the suffering of soldiers at the Battle of Solferino.

Three years later he published a pamphlet urging the formation of a voluntary society to care for the wounded in wartime. The result was the formation of the Red Cross.

LUCKY LOCALS

The healthiest soldiers in the British army in the mid-1800s were more often than not the locally recruited sepoys (native infantry) who served in India. They had a natural immunity to many of the illnesses that killed their British comrades.

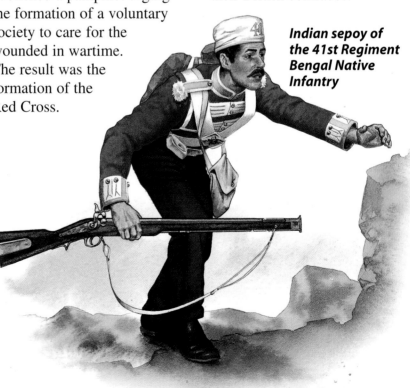

Indian sepoy of the 41st Regiment Bengal Native Infantry

WAR NEWS

After the Battle of the Alma in the Crimea in 1854, a courier carried word of the British victory overland to the nearest telegraph station, hundreds of kilometres away. It took ten days for the message to get to where it could be sent to London. Later in the war the telegraph was extended and news was only hours away from Europe.

By the time of the American Civil War there was an extensive network of telegraph wires in the United States, which was widely used by both sides. And by that time most newspapers employed war correspondents.

People in London read reports of the Crimean War in **The Times** *newspaper.*

Confederate troops lay a telegraph wire.

RISKY BUSINESS

During the Napoleonic War a journalist called Henry Crabbe Robinson sent letters to *The Times* newspaper, reporting British victories and French defeats. But it was not until the Crimean War, when *The Times* sent journalist William Howard Russell to the Crimea, that war reporting really began.

TELEGRAPH LINES

The fastest way for messages to get through in the 19th century was by telegraph. A sender tapped out pulses of electric current with a metal key. The pulses travelled along wires, creating a coded pattern of dots and dashes. The dots and dashes were decoded to reveal the message or report.

CRIMEAN HORROR

In the Crimea, Russell did more than simply tell his readers which side won which battle. His reports on the conditions the soldiers faced horrified readers.

The British army issued Russell with a pass to allow him access to British trenches during the war.

An extract from Russell's report on the Crimea:

'The men suffered exceedingly from cold. Some of them had no beds to lie on and none had more than their single regulation blanket. They dressed to go to bed, putting on all their spare clothing before they tried to sleep.'

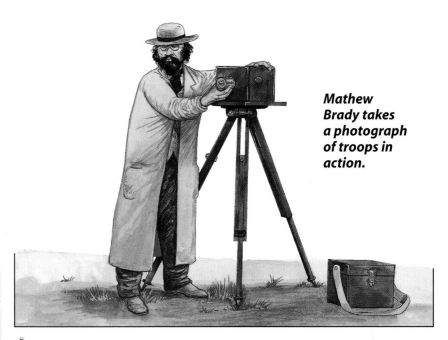

Mathew Brady takes a photograph of troops in action.

PHOTOGRAPHING THE ACTION

During the US Civil War, Mathew Brady, an American photographer, received permission from President Lincoln to photograph army units. By the end of the war, he and his team had taken more than 3,500 photographs, many of them taken in terrible conditions. There are scenes of battle and individual soldiers whose faces, haunted by the horrors of war, still stare at us from 150 years ago.

Photograph of Union troops by Mathew Brady, 1864

GLOSSARY

Artillery
The large guns of an army and the men who maintain and fire them.

The Balkans
The large peninsula in South-east Europe, between the Adriatic and Aegean Seas.

Bolt
A sliding bar in a breech-loading firearm that ejects a spent cartridge and guides a new one into the breech.

Breech-loader
A gun that is loaded in a chamber at the stock end of the barrel.

British East India Company
The company that effectively ran India on behalf of the British government until shortly after the Indian Mutiny.

Cannon
Non-portable firearm with a long barrel and a calibre of more than 20 mm.

Carbine
A short, light gun, originally designed to be used by soldiers on horseback.

Cavalry
The mounted soldiers of an army.

Commission
The document that gives an officer authority to perform military duty.

Union general

Confederate States
The southern states of the USA that broke away from the others in 1860, precipitating the Civil War.

Conscription
Compulsory military service, often, but not necessarily, in times of war.

Crimea
A peninsula in Russia between the Black Sea and the Sea of Azov.

Fusilier
A private soldier in a British rifle regiment.

Guardsman
A private soldier in a British Guards regiment.

Gunner
A private soldier in Britain's Royal Regiment of Artillery.

Grapeshot
Cannon ammunition consisting of a cluster of small iron balls separated by wooden discs. The balls scatter after firing.

Infantry
The foot soldiers of an army.

Kepi
A military cap with a circular top and a horizontal peak.

Militiamen
Civilians who volunteer for military training to provide a home defence force and to swell army numbers in wartime.

Musket
A long-barrelled, muzzle-loading shoulder gun in service from c.1650 to the mid-1800s.

Muzzle-loader
A gun in which the ammunition is loaded by being pushed down the barrel via the muzzle.

Napoleonic Wars
The wars fought by France under the leadership of Napoleon Bonaparte against Britain and her allies from 1800-15.

Officer
A soldier above the rank of regimental sergeant major.

Private
The lowest rank in any army.

Prussia
The most powerful German state in the 19th century and the driving force behind unifying all independent German states into one country.

Ramrod
A wooden or iron rod used to push ammunition into the barrel of a gun.

Regiment
A large, permanent military unit, usually comprising a number of battalions and often further divided into companies and platoons.

Sabre
A long, curved, single-edged sword designed for use on horseback.

Shako
A peaked cap, also known as a 'stovepipe', worn by soldiers of many countries throughout the 19th century until the introduction of the helmet (in Britain, around 1878).

British soldier loading his musket

Shell
Hollow artillery ammunition either filled with explosives primed to explode during flight, on impact or on penetration, or with pieces of shrapnel.

Shrapnel
A shell containing a number of small pellets or bullets that explode before impact. The fragments that such a shell contains.

Telegraph
A system by which information is transmitted over a long distance by using coded electric signals sent along a transmission wire and connected to a receiving instrument.

INDEX

PHOTOGRAPHIC CREDITS
Peter Newark's American Pictures pp.22, 29
Peter Newark's Military Pictures pp.10, 17, 24, 26